Lerner SPORTS

I0866939

DALE EARNHARDT JR.
RACING ROYALTY

TRACY SUE WALKER

LERNER PUBLICATIONS ◆ MINNEAPOLIS

Copyright © 2023 by Lerner Publishing Group, Inc.

All rights reserved. International copyright secured. No part of this book may be reproduced, stored in a retrieval system, or transmitted in any form or by any means—electronic, mechanical, photocopying, recording, or otherwise—without the prior written permission of Lerner Publishing Group, Inc., except for the inclusion of brief quotations in an acknowledged review.

Lerner Publications Company
An imprint of Lerner Publishing Group, Inc.
241 First Avenue North
Minneapolis, MN 55401 USA

For reading levels and more information, look up this title at www.lernerbooks.com.

Main body text set in Myriad Pro Semibold. Typeface provided by Adobe.

Editor: Matt Doeden **Photo Editor:** Annie Zheng

Library of Congress Cataloging-in-Publication Data

Names: Walker, Tracy Sue, author.
Title: Dale Earnhardt Jr. : racing royalty / Tracy Sue Walker.
Description: Minneapolis, MN : Lerner Publications, [2023] | Series: Epic Sports Bios (Lerner Sports) | Includes bibliographical references and index. | Audience: Ages 7–11 years | Audience: Grades 4–6 | Summary: "Dale Earnhardt Jr. rose from his father's shadow to become one of the greatest drivers in stock car racing. He holds 26 wins in the NASCAR Cup Series and is a two-time winner of the Daytona 500. Follow the life and career of NASCAR's biggest star"— Provided by publisher.
Identifiers: LCCN 2022013919 (print) | LCCN 2022013920 (ebook) | ISBN 9781728476506 (Library Binding) | ISBN 9781728478548 (Paperback) | ISBN 9781728482460 (eBook)
Subjects: LCSH: Earnhardt, Dale, Jr.—Juvenile literature. | Automobile racing drivers—United States—Biography—Juvenile literature.
Classification: LCC GV1032.E19 W35 2023 (print) | LCC GV1032.E19 (ebook) | DDC 796.72092 [B]—dc23/eng/20220405

LC record available at https://lccn.loc.gov/2022013919
LC ebook record available at https://lccn.loc.gov/2022013920

Manufactured in the United States of America
1-52231-50671-7/18/2022

TABLE OF CONTENTS

DAYTONA CHAMPION

Race car drivers revved their engines. Dale Earnhardt Jr. gripped his steering wheel. As the green flag waved, his number 8 Chevrolet roared down the track. The 2004 Daytona 500, NASCAR's biggest race of the season, was underway. Who would win?

Dale Earnhardt Jr. celebrates with his team after the 2004 Daytona 500. It was the first Daytona 500 victory of his career.

FACTS AT A GLANCE

Date of birth: October 10, 1974

Position: driver

League: NASCAR

Professional highlights: selected a record 15 times as NASCAR's Most Popular Driver; had 26 career wins; won the Daytona 500 in 2004 and 2014

Personal highlights: only third-generation NASCAR champion; married to Amy Earnhardt, with two daughters; inducted into the NASCAR Hall of Fame in January 2022

Earnhardt dives to the inside lane as he passes Tony Stewart for the lead in the 2004 Daytona 500.

With 19 laps to go, Earnhardt was close behind leader Tony Stewart. Earnhardt quickly dove down to the inner part of the track. With a burst of speed, he pulled even with Stewart. The two rode side by side until Earnhardt finally made the pass.

No one came close to Earnhardt in the final laps of the race. He crossed the finish line in first place. The crowd stood and cheered wildly.

It was Earnhardt's first Daytona 500 victory. His win came three years after his father, Dale Earnhardt Sr., was killed on the race's final lap. Earnhardt said that he felt as though his dad was riding with him. "It's just the greatest race," he said. "It's the greatest day of my life. I can't really describe it."

Fans cheer for Earnhardt as confetti rains down on him after the 2004 Daytona 500.

RACING IN THE BLOOD

Ralph Dale Earnhardt Jr. was born on October 10, 1974, in North Carolina. His grandfather, Ralph Earnhardt, was a famous short track driver. His father, Dale Earnhardt Sr., was a NASCAR champion. Dale Jr. dreamed of becoming a driver too.

Earnhardt rides in the inside lane during a Legends race in the early 1990s.

Dale Jr. (*top left*) celebrates his dad's 1990 Cup championship after a race at Atlanta Motor Speedway.

He was interested in cars from an early age. This interest grew as he got older. After high school, Earnhardt attended Mitchell Community College in Statesville, North Carolina. He studied automotive repair. He also went to a race car driving school where he learned techniques and strategies.

RACING FLAGS

In NASCAR, a signaler sits on a platform above the start/finish line. They wave flags to signal the race conditions to drivers. The green flag signals the start of a race or a restart after a caution. A yellow flag signals caution. The checkered flag signals the end of the race.

His father wanted him to earn his own way as a driver. "Anybody who was around when I was a kid knows that Dad never handed me a thing," Earnhardt said. "He was real careful about that."

He began racing Legends cars—small replicas of old cars. In October 1992, Earnhardt scored his first win at Charlotte Motor Speedway.

PEDAL TO THE METAL

Earnhardt's chance to prove he was ready for a higher level of racing came soon. In June 1996, he qualified for the Carolina Pride 250 race in Myrtle Beach, South Carolina. The race was part of NASCAR's Xfinity Series, its second level of stock car racing. It's where many drivers prepare for NASCAR's highest level of stock car racing.

Earnhardt climbs out of his Xfinity Series car after a 1999 race. Xfinity Series cars are lighter and less powerful than Cup cars.

Earnhardt finished 14th in the race. His dad was impressed. He offered his son a chance to drive a car in the Xfinity Series for his race team, Dale Earnhardt, Inc.

The younger Earnhardt claimed his first Xfinity Series win at Texas Motor Speedway on April 4, 1998. The crowd cheered as he crossed the finish line. His teammates celebrated. His father even had tears in his eyes.

Earnhardt drove the number 3 car in his first full season in NASCAR's Xfinity Series.

Left to right: Dale Earnhardt Sr.; his wife, Teresa Earnhardt; his daughter Kelley; and Dale Earnhardt Jr. with the 1998 Xfinity Series trophy that Dale Earnhardt Jr. won

Earnhardt had several more wins in 1998. He moved into first place in the points standings. "Winning races is a great bonus," he said, "but the championship is the main focus."

Earnhardt kept up his good performance. He won the 1998 championship by 48 points over second-place Matt Kenseth. It was a huge accomplishment for a rookie. It also made him NASCAR's first third-generation champion, after his father and grandfather.

CUP RACING

Earnhardt's goal was to race in NASCAR's top level, the Cup Series. In 1999, he got his chance. He signed a deal to drive for Dale Earnhardt, Inc. He took over the number 8 car for a partial Cup schedule that year. Meanwhile, he continued to excel in the Xfinity Series. He won a second straight championship.

Earnhardt drove the number 8 car for Dale Earnhardt, Inc.

Dale Earnhardt Jr. (*right*) poses with his dad at a race in 2001.

Cup racing was new for Earnhardt. The cars were heavier and faster. Cup races were usually twice the length of Xfinity Series races. Earnhardt struggled to get used to Cup racing. His best finish in 1999 was 10th place.

In 2000, Earnhardt ran a full Cup schedule. His dad had a huge fan following in NASCAR. That made the younger Earnhardt an instant fan favorite. People flocked to races wearing hats and shirts with his name on them. But others criticized him. They felt he had a full-time ride only because of his father's success. All eyes were on the young driver. That came with a lot of pressure.

Dale Earnhardt Jr. is among the drivers awaiting the green flag before the 2000 Daytona 500.

Earnhardt was the top qualifying rookie for the Daytona 500. When race day arrived, he remained close to the front for most of the race. He finished in 13th place.

That year Earnhardt won his first Winston Cup race at the DirecTV 500 at Texas Motor Speedway. The crowd roared as he pulled his car to Victory Lane. His father even stuck his head inside his son's car to congratulate him.

Earnhardt in 2000, the year he earned his first Cup Series victory

NASCAR'S BIGGEST RACE

NASCAR's first race of the season, the Daytona 500, is also its biggest. It is also called the Great American Race. The days leading up to the Daytona 500 are called Speedweeks. Drivers take part in a series of qualifying laps and short "duel" races to decide their starting positions.

Earnhardt's early success didn't last. He struggled in the second half of the 2000 season. He didn't even earn a single top 10 finish. The disappointing finish left him 16th in the Cup standings.

"I don't doubt my ability to be a winner," he said. "And until it happens again, I learn more about how to handle losing."

Earnhardt qualified sixth for the 2001 Daytona 500. He stayed near the front for most of the race. On the final lap, Earnhardt was in second place behind his teammate Michael Waltrip.

A huge crash started just behind Earnhardt. One of the drivers in the crash was his dad. His number 3 car slammed hard into the wall.

Waltrip crossed the finish line first, with Earnhardt close behind. Meanwhile, medical crews rushed to the crash. Fans looked on nervously as the crews gathered around the elder Earnhardt's car.

An ambulance rushed him to the hospital. A few hours later, NASCAR president Mike Helton made a difficult announcement. Dale Earnhardt Sr. had died in the crash. After years in his father's shadow, suddenly, Earnhardt felt very alone.

Fans pay tribute to Dale Earnhardt Sr. after his death in 2001.

MOVING FORWARD

On July 7, 2001, NASCAR returned to Daytona for the first time since the crash. Earnhardt went on to win the race. He was thankful to have something to celebrate.

A month later, Earnhardt won the EA Sports 500 at Talladega Superspeedway in Alabama. The win lifted him to fifth in the Cup standings. But Earnhardt again faded late in the season.

Earnhardt raises his arms after a 2002 victory at Talladega Superspeedway.

He finished in 11th place. The 2003 season gave Earnhardt the chance to realize his goal of having consistent finishes. But even though he had many top-five finishes, he still wasn't winning.

He was winning in the hearts of fans, though. That year Earnhardt was voted NASCAR's Most Popular Driver. He received more votes than the next 10 drivers combined.

Earnhardt signs autographs for fans.

GAMER

Earnhardt loves playing video games, but it's not just for fun. Racing games help him practice driving. In 2004, he and teammate Martin Truex Jr. used a video game strategy at a real race in Talladega. It worked on the track, and Truex won the race.

CHASING DREAMS

In 2008, Earnhardt made a bold move. He left Dale Earnhardt, Inc., to sign with Hendrick Motorsports. Hendrick was one of NASCAR's strongest teams. Earnhardt took over the team's number 88 car.

Earnhardt stands with his car before the final Cup race of 2017.

NASCAR champion Jeff Gordon speaks with Earnhardt at a 2006 race. While many fans considered Gordon and Earnhardt rivals, they went on to become teammates.

Fans weren't sure what to think of the move. Earnhardt was joining forces with Jeff Gordon. Gordon had long been his father's biggest rival. Many of Earnhardt's fans rooted against Gordon.

Earnhardt believed that the move to Hendrick Motorsports gave him the best chance to compete. And while many of his fans thought of Hendrick as a rival, he didn't see it that way. For Earnhardt, team owner Rick Hendrick was someone he looked up to. "I've always daydreamed about driving for Rick since I started to drive racecars," Earnhardt said. "I guess if I had my choice in a perfect world, he was kind of always in the lead."

Earnhardt continued giving all he had to racing, even when luck wasn't on his side. He finished second five times in 2013 but had no wins. When he entered the 2014 Daytona 500, it was with a 55-race winless streak. But his luck was about to change.

Drivers had completed 38 laps when storms swept across the track. The race was halted. More than six hours passed before they were allowed back on the track. In the final minutes of the race, Earnhardt avoided a huge crash and made a two-lap dash for the win. It was his first Daytona 500 win since 2004.

Earnhardt's win at the 2014 Daytona 500 came a decade after his first win in the Great American Race.

Earnhardt navigates a turn in a 2016 race at Phoenix International Raceway.

In 2016, Earnhardt faced a difficult season. He didn't compete in the second half, because he was recovering from a concussion. The following year, Earnhardt decided to step away from the sport. He wanted to spend more time with his wife and two daughters.

To honor his fans, teammates, and sponsors, he began a five-month appreciation campaign called JR Nation Appreci88ion Tour. It lasted the rest of the 2017 season. It included many opportunities for fan engagement and to celebrate his career.

Earnhardt remained NASCAR's Most Popular Driver through 2017, the final season of his career.

Even though Earnhardt retired from full-time NASCAR racing, he didn't leave the sport. He became a team owner with JR Motorsports. In 2018, he joined the NBC television network's broadcast team as a race commentator.

Earnhardt continues to concentrate on his businesses and on the Dale Jr. Foundation. This charity helps young people improve their education, confidence, and goal setting. He is also involved in the Make-A-Wish Foundation, which grants wishes to seriously ill children.

Earnhardt never met his goal of winning a Cup championship. But his ability to connect with his fans make him one of the most popular figures in the sport, even long after his retirement.

SIGNIFICANT STATS

Xfinity Series championships: 2 (1998, 1999)

Cup Series races: 631

Cup Series wins: 26

Cup Series laps run: 179,429

Cup Series laps led: 8,234

Cup Series poles: 15

Highest season finish: 3 (2003)

Times chosen Most Popular Driver: 15

GLOSSARY

caution: a race condition during which the track is unsafe for racing speeds. Wrecks, debris, and weather are common causes.

concussion: a brain injury

green flag: a flag waved to start a race and restart a race after a caution

Legends: small race cars built as replicas of larger cars

qualifying: determining a race's starting order

retire: to end a career

rookie: a first-year driver

series: a group of races that, put together, make up a racing season

sponsor: a company that pays to advertise

strategy: a plan for achieving a goal

SOURCE NOTES

7 Kathy Persinger, *Dale Earnhardt Jr.: Born to Race* (Champaign, IL: Sports Publishing, 2001), 22.

10 Larry Cothren, *Earnhardt: A Racing Family Legacy* (St. Paul: Motorbooks, 2003), 221.

13 "NASCAR—Earnhardt Jr. Wins Busch Race," RaceLink.com, July 20, 1998, http://www.racelink.com/rl_news/archive/0798/drn_week4.html (site discontinued).

18 Dale Earnhardt Jr. and Jade Gurss, *Driver #8* (New York: Warner Books, 2002), 248.

23 David Newton, "Earnhardt to Join Gordon, Johnson in Hendrick Stable," ESPN.com, June 13, 2007, https://www.espn.com/racing/news/story?id=2902693&seriesId=2.

LEARN MORE

Levit, Joe. *Auto Racing's G.O.A.T.: Dale Earnhardt, Jimmie Johnson, and More*. Minneapolis: Lerner Publications, 2020.

NASCAR
https://www.nascar.com

NASCAR Hall of Fame
https://www.nascarhall.com

Official Website of Dale Earnhardt Jr.
https://www.dalejr.com

Reinke, Beth Bence. *Superfast Stock Car Racing*. Minneapolis: Lerner Publications, 2020.

Stabler, David. *Who Is Dale Earnhardt Jr.?* New York: Penguin Workshop, 2022.

INDEX

PHOTO ACKNOWLEDGMENTS

Image credits: AP Photo/Terry Renna, pp. 4, 6, 7; stockphoto-graf/Shutterstock, pp. 5, 28; RacingOne/ISC Images & Archives/Getty Images, pp. 8, 12; Brian Cleary/Getty Images Sport/Getty Images, p. 9; Sporting News/Getty Images, p. 11; RacingOne/ISC Archives/CQ-Roll Call Group/Getty Images, pp. 13, 15; Robert Laberge/Getty Images Sport/Getty Images, p. 14; David Madison/Getty Images Sport/Getty Images, p. 16; AP Photo/Wayne Scarberry, p. 17; Erik Perel/Stringer/AFP/Getty Images, p. 19; AP Photo/Dave Martin, p. 20; Dimitrios Kambouris/WireImage/Getty Images, p. 21; AP Photo/Nigel Kinrade/NKP, pp. 22, 26; Worth Canoy/Icon Sportswire/Getty Images, p. 23; Grindstone Media Group/Shutterstock, p. 24; action sports/Shutterstock, p. 25.

Design elements: saicle/iStock/Getty Images.

Cover: AP Photo/Butch Dill (bottom); Grindstone Media Group/Shutterstock (top).